Grafting Fruit Trees

Grafting for Fruit Trees

Larry Southwick

CONTENTS

Introduction

The term *graft* stems from the words *greffe* or *grafe* or *graphium*, referring to the pencil shape of a scion or shoot. Grafting is the act of joining two plant parts so that they unite or grow together to achieve a desired result.

The grafting of fruit trees is one of the oldest of recorded horticultural practices, and was mentioned by Theophrastus about 300 BC. The Romans developed and utilized several grafting techniques that are still in use today. In China as early as the fourth century AD, it was reported that Oriental pear was "best suited" to the rootstock Tu Li, indicating that other combinations were less successful. Also, Japanese plum was found to be successfully grafted onto peach but not vice versa. Thus many of the principles of grafting were known around the world in very early times.

A.J. Downing discussed grafting in his book The Fruits and Fruit Trees of America published in 1857 and stated: "No person having any interest in a garden should be unable to perform these operations, as they are capable of effecting transformations and improvements in all trees and shrubs."

Actually, grafting and budding are not difficult. A little knowledge about the techniques helps to inject more fun into the procedures, especially since know-how will almost guarantee success.

Definition of Terms

Grafting
The practice of physically joining parts of two individual plants, as with stock and scion, so that they will form a union and grow together.

Budding
A form of grafting, where a single bud is used instead of a piece of wood (shoot) containing several buds.

Scion
Piece of shoot to be grafted or is already grafted into the stock. It usually is dormant wood of the previous season's shoot growth. From it grows a branch or a whole tree. The varietal characteristics of the scion (for example McIntosh apple) are thus perpetuated. They are not changed by the stock to which the scion is joined.

Bud
That portion of a shoot or scion found at the base of each leaf stalk. Buds for propagation may be taken in midsummer or later. This is when budding is done. The bud then grows out the next season and forms a new branch or whole tree, perpetuating the variety the same as the scion in grafting.

Stock
The root, branch, or tree trunk into which a graft or bud is set; that part of the tree below the point of insertion of the scion or bud; below the graft union.

Cambium
Thin layer of active cells between the bark and the wood which produces new bark on the outside and new wood on the inside. When bark is "slipped" or pulled off a shoot or branch, the slippage commonly is at the cambium layer. This layer of living and dividing cells is the source of growth, thus increasing the thickness of a woody stem, and causing annual growth rings. Obviously, its preservation is essential. The cambium cells of scion and stock must unite to result in successful grafting and budding. Since growth takes place in the cambium region, it is essential to bring the cambial tissue of both stock and scion (or bud) into contact with each

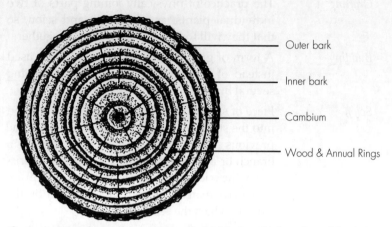

Outer bark

Inner bark

Cambium

Wood & Annual Rings

Cross-section of a stock or scion or limb showing the location of the important cambium layer.

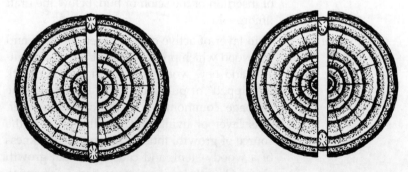

Cross-sections, looking down on cleft grafts. On left, scions are wrongly placed since the cambiums of scion and stock are not in contact, although the outside surfaces or edges are flush or even. The stock bark is thicker. On right, note that scions are in far enough that the cambium layer contacts the cambium of the stock.

other so that subsequent growth will form a continuous layer of new wood uniting the parts as one.

Graft or Bud Union
Area of attachment between the scion (or bud) and the stock. This usually is easily discernable for a year or more after grafting or budding, like a healed wound on people which may leave a visible scar.

Compatible
The scion (or bud) and the stock (if compatible) are able to form a successful union wherein the vascular elements of both scion and stock are dovetailed strongly together. Incompatibility has been defined as the characteristic interruption in cambial and vascular continuity which leads to smooth breaks at the point of union, thereby making the union unsuccessful. Grafting normally is confined to closely related plants, for example, one variety of apple on another, or pear on pear, or dogwood on dogwood. Apple cannot be grafted successfully on peach or pear or vice versa and therefore they are considered incompatible. The same is true with pear on cherry, apple on cherry, pear on peach, peach on cherry, etc. Incompatible combinations exhibit one or more of the following: low percentage of success, premature autumn leaf coloration, premature flowerbud formation, early leaf fall, dying back of young shoots, mechanically weak unions, increased winter injury. In a few cases, grafting can be accomplished with different genera such as apple *(Malus)* on pear *(Pyrus)* and pear on quince *(Cydonia)* but this is not common.

Dormant
Usually refers to the condition of vegetative tissues (shoots and buds) during the period when no vegetative growth takes place, as in winter. Buds also may be dormant on new growing shoots and may remain dormant until the next spring when they resume growth.

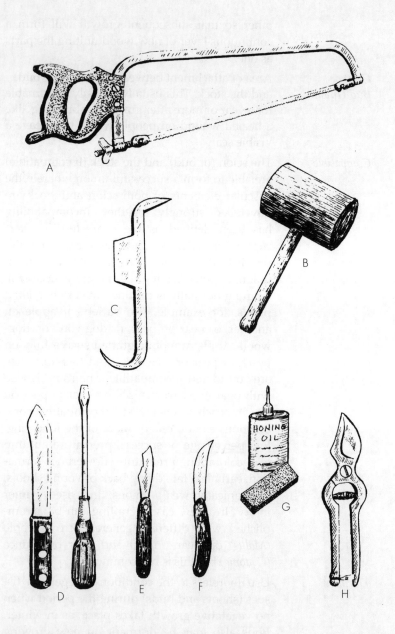

Tools used in grafting and budding:
A-saw, B-mallet, C-grafting tool, D-heavy knife and screw driver can sub-
stitute for C, E-budding knife, F-knife for tub and side grafting, G-hand
hone or tool for sharpening knives, H-pruning shears

Tools for Grafting

Grafting can be done with very little equipment such as a saw, knife, pruning shears, screwdriver, small brads (nails), and hand grafting wax. A more complete set of tools is illustrated. It is essential that cutting tools are sharp.

By far the most important grafting tool is a sharp knife. It should have a thin blade as well as a sharp edge. It can be an ordinary pocket knife or a specialized budding knife.

Pruning saws and pruning shears are available at local hardware stores. Saws may be curved and are designed to cut green wood cleanly and smoothly. The author has found Sears Craftsman pruning saw, with Kromedge blade, easy to use. Other types such as bow saws or even a carpenter's saw can be effective as long as they are sharp and shiny. Pruning shears of the bypass style are more universally used than the snap-cut style (cutting blade presses down onto a flat surface) but either is all right if sharp and especially not rusty. Special budding and grafting knives are not really necessary for a little backyard grafting and budding. A pocket knife can suffice as long as it is sharp. A hand hone is very useful for putting a good edge on knives. A large screwdriver can substitute for the grafting tool illustrated and a piece of wood or carpenter's hammer can be substituted for a specialized wooden mallet.

Wound Dressing

Dressings are not only desirable but are necessary to prevent drying and subsequent death of tissues and therefore the failure of the graft. Wax or other dressing should be applied immediately after the grafting operation.

The United States Department of Agriculture recommends asphalt-water emulsion dressing as protective coating in grafting operations. These emulsions, available from seedsmen and garden supply stores, can be thinned with water, can be applied cold, will adhere to fresh wounds, do not crack with changes in temperature, and dry rapidly. An example of a good product is Tanglefoot Grafting Compound and Wound Dressing by Tanglefoot Company, Grand Rapids, Michigan.

Horticultural waxes are also available and can be kneaded by hand and warmed for easier use. Linseed or other vegetable oil on the hands facilitates handling these wax dressings. I have used these waxes successfully as long as they are warm and pliable and are carefully applied. They are available at garden stores in small packages. A good product is Trowbridge Grafting Wax, manufactured by Walter E. Clark & Son, Orange, Connecticut. The one-pound package contains directions for hand and brush use.

Common ingredients of homemade waxes are rosin, beeswax, and tallow. One formula is four parts rosin, two parts beeswax and one part tallow slowly melted together, but not boiled, and thoroughly mixed. After cooling, often in cold water, the wax is pulled, in the same manner as taffy, until it becomes straw-colored and uniform in texture. Before pulling, it is best to grease the hands with tallow or linseed oil. When wax is ready to use it may be stored in rolls in waxed paper.

Why Graft?

The home orchardist may or may not want to utilize grafting and budding. These procedures are useful in case a person wishes to change varieties on trees now growing on his place, instead of removing unwanted trees and planting new ones. Also, two or more varieties of apple, for example, may be desired on a single tree, and this is possible via grafting or budding on existing trees.

There is no limit as to the number of varieties of apple, for example, that can be grown on a single tree. This is determined by the whim of the grafter or budder. Usually, however, two or three varieties provide an adequate "mixed tree" curiosity for a home orchard. Several kinds of fruits on a single tree may be wanted, but cannot be achieved because of the compatibility factor.

Many persons ask me about renewal of old and even decrepit trees by grafting. In many cases, old trees are just that and rejuvenation efforts have small chance of success. Topworking should be limited to younger and healthy trees. However, scion wood and buds from good shoot growth on older trees are just as good for grafting and budding as similar scions or buds from younger trees. Tree age is not the criterion; the condition of the wood is.

Another reason for grafting is the saving of trees that have been girdled at or near the base by mice or rabbits chewing on the bark, or the lower bark has been injured by winter injury, mechanical damage, or sun scald. This will be discussed further under Bridge Grafting.

A final reason is that it can be fun to manipulate nature to suit a need or a whim. Grafting is utilitarian and stimulating. As a youth, I experimented with grafting of sunflowers, often quite successfully, and with grafting apples and pears on wild thornapples or hawthorn (*Crataegus* spp.) and on wild apple trees growing along stone walls and fencerows on the family farm.

Some of these grafts, often crudely done, grew successfully and these afforded considerable satisfaction to a budding horticulturist. The hawthorn and wild apple thus became the stocks on which useful apple varieties were grown to bear edible and desirable fruit. A mission was accomplished. I must admit that these graft unions were not wholly compatible and often were not long-lived, even though "successful."

Types of Grafts

Grafts can be classified in two ways, according to position of the scion on the stock and according to type of cut and purpose. In the first classification, there are root, crown, stem and top grafts. In the second, there are cleft, bridge, bark, saddle, veneer, side, inlay, and whip grafts. Budding is a variation of grafting. The more important of these to the home orchardist will be discussed here.

When to Graft or Bud

Grafting usually is done in spring just before growth starts. This means before leaf and flower buds start to grow. There is a period of three to four weeks of good grafting weather, typically warm days and cool nights. The sap is moving, the bark "slips" easily, and the winter buds are gearing up for spring growth, but do not yet show new growth.

Grafting can be done after growth begins but in any case the scion wood used must be dormant. Scion wood can be cut in late winter or early spring and kept dormant by storing in a refrigerator. On the other hand, budding is performed in summer, normally from mid-July through August, when new buds are mature or dormant on current shoot growth.

Source of Scion and Bud Wood

Usually, the home gardener can obtain scions and buds from his own trees or from his neighbor's trees. Twigs that have made growth of one to two feet the preceding season usually furnish the best scion wood. The buds should be plump and mature. The mid-portion to the one-year growth makes the best scions. For certain desirable older varieties that one may want, it may be necessary to contact a nursery or a special source such as the Tower Hill Botanic Garden, 30 Tower Hill Road, Boylston, Massachusetts 01505. They may make a small charge. A good source of some old and many new introductions is the New York State Fruit Testing Association, Geneva, New York 14456.

When scion wood is shopped, it must be wrapped properly to keep it moist. When received, remove packing and place in a refrigerator (not the freezing compartment) in moist toweling, sphagnum or sawdust. Scion wood must be moist and "alive" when it is used for grafting. It makes no difference whether buds or scions are taken from full-sized or from dwarf trees; the results will be equal provided the buds and scions are of proper vigor, are taken at the right time, and are protected from drying out prior to use.

Cleft Grafting

This procedure is useful to change apple or pear trees from one variety to another or to add varieties on single trees. Changing the entire top of a tree to one or more different varieties is called top-working. Mature trees may be topworked but the older the tree and the larger the branches the more difficult is the task. The most successful grafting of older trees is done on healthy branches not over 2 inches in diameter. There is no sense in trying to topwork decrepit older trees (twenty years of so) with broken branches and evidence of wood rot and general deterioration. Water sprouts often grow on limbs pruned back for grafting and should be cut back, especially during the first year after topworking.

Cleft grafting is less successful on stone fruits such as peaches and plums. With these fruits, budding in midsummer can be used on one- or two-year-old wood, as discussed later, to accomplish the same purpose.

The branch to be grafted should be 1 to 2 inches in diameter. It is cut off square, vertical to the growth, and the stub is split

Cleft grafting:
A-prepared scions, B-cambium layers of scions contact cambium zone of stock, C-cut-away to show scions in place, D-side view, E-waxed graft

2 to 3 inches deep with a grafting chisel or similar tool as in the illustration. To facilitate splitting and insertion of scions, the branch should be cut at least eight inches beyond its junction with another branch.

The scions are prepared by making long, sloping cuts from 1½ to 2 inches in length on both sides of the lower ends. The cut scion should be *slightly* thicker on the outside than the inside. The scion is usually 4 or 5 inches long and should have two or three buds above the beveled cuts. The split stub is pried open and the scions inserted at both sides *so that the cambiums of the scions and stub meet.* If the scion is placed just inside the outer bark and the top tilted outward very slightly, this vital contact is practically assured. Unless the cambiums meet, there will be no union. Grafting wax or asphalt-water emulsion dressing is then applied to the cut surface of the stub and to the scion tips.

After the first season's growth, save the more vigorous scion growth (if they both grew) and prune back the other to two or three buds. Continue to prune this second scion so that the first one assumes full growth and dominance. When the wound has healed, cut back the repressed scion completely.

Left scion prepared with blunt end gives better cambium contact and stability than scion on right beveled to a point.

Bark Graft

In this graft, the branch is cut but instead of splitting the stub, only the bark is split down for a distance of two or three inches and the corners separated enough to permit insertion of the scion which is prepared by making a slanting cut on *one* side about 1 to 1½ inch in length. The scion is then pushed downward under the bark until the lower bud is about even with the cut surface of the tub. Two No. 20 gauge ¾-inch flathead nails or small brads are driven into each scion to hold it firmly in place. Waxing protection finishes the job.

Scions may be placed three to four inches apart around the stub. This graft exposes less wood than the cleft graft thus requiring less wax, and it can be used on larger stubs, three to four inches in diameter. It is also useful on cherries and other stone fruits. As in

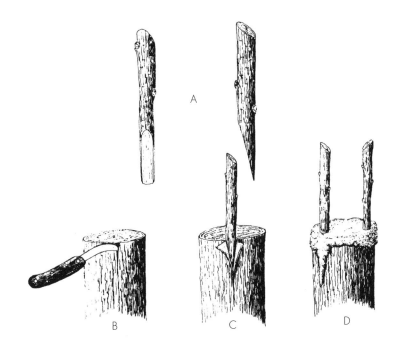

Bark graft:
A-scion, B-splitting bark, C-one scion inserted, D-job completed including waxing

cleft grafting, save only one scion for the permanent branch, keeping the others pruned back and finally eliminating them.

Inlay Graft
(also called Veneer and Rind)

This is similar to the bark graft except that a *rectangular* shaped piece of bark is cut out of the stub and the scion is cut to fit.

Be sure to remove any inner light green bark if it does not come off when the piece of bark is removed. Otherwise, the cambium on the tub will be covered and contact with the scion cambium will not be made. If this happens, uniting of the two parts is prevented by a physical barrier. Nails are used and scions should be spaced three to four inches apart, as in bark grafting large limbs.

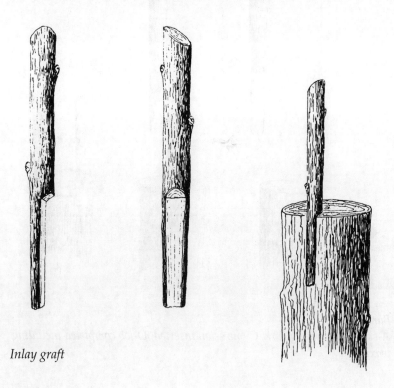

Inlay graft

Bridge Graft

Bridge grafting is the bridging of a bark-girdled area of a tree trunk by grafting into the good bark above and below the injury in order to re-establish sap flow and connection between root and top. Girdling of fruit trees may be caused by rabbits, mice, sun scald, winter injury, disease, or mechanical injury. Girdled trees must be "bridged" if they are to be salvaged. Otherwise they will die. There must be an active or live connection between the top and the root of any plant.

Usually the cause of girdling in the backyard orchard is the chewing of the bark during the winter under the protection of snow

Young dwarf apple tree bridged by author in April 1976 following winter bark girdling by rabbits. This photo was taken in July 1978. The tree had a good crop of apples that year.

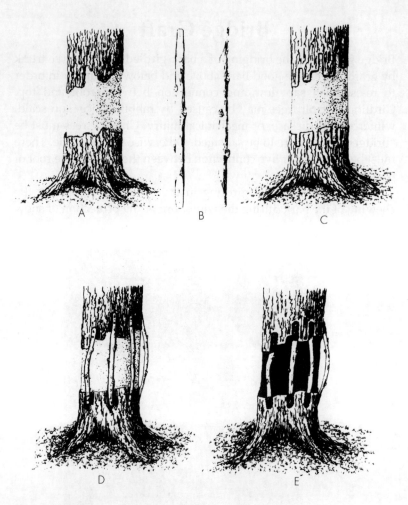

Bridge grafting:
A-shows bark girdled area, B-scions, C-channels made, D-scions in place,
E-wounds covered

cover by field mice. Pine mice usually girdle trees under the ground. Cottontail rabbits also girdle small trees but mostly chew off the top twigs and shoots above the snow line.

Scions are placed via bark grafting in the spring as soon as bark lifts (slips) freely from the wood. Here again the scion wood must be dormant and preferably should have been collected two to four weeks earlier and kept moist and refrigerated.

The channel or inlay graft method is preferred for bridging. The scions are prepared as shown in illustrations and are cut long enough to bridge the injured area. They should be equal in diameter to a lead pencil for small trees and up to a half-inch in diameter for larger trees. It is usually a wasted effort to try to bridge large wounds with small, puny scion wood. Each end is beheveled on the side opposite the natural bow of the wood if any. When scions are cut to the proper length and beveled for two to three inches at each end, they are laid over the wound in the positions they are to be placed. By marking around the ends with a knife point for the channels to be cut in the bark, both above and below, good fits of the scions in the channels should result.

The distance between the ends of the channels in the bark on the stem or trunk should be slightly less than the length of the scions to allow for a slight outward bow of the scions. This allows better contact of the scions and stock cambium and reduces the hazard of breakage from trees swaying in the wind.

The channels are made by removing the strips of bark after cutting along the lines marked around the scions. These strips should come away easily from the wood, indicating good cambial cell activity. If it resists, postpone bridging until it peels easily. If it still does not peel, the channel should be made in another place where the bark is in better condition.

Place the lower end of the scion in position and nail to the wood with small brads. Then spring the upper end into position and nail again. Place scions about three to four inches apart. Cover all wounded surfaces and areas with grafting wax or asphalt-water emulsion dressing.

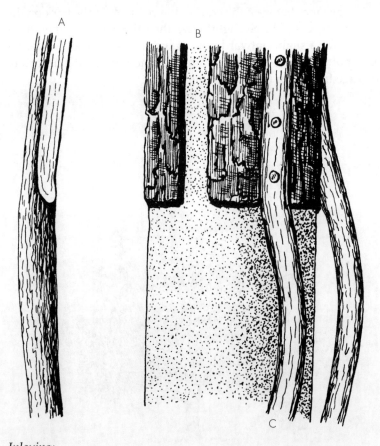

Inlaying:
A-scion cut and shaped, B-slot or channel cut in bark of tree the same width as the scion, C-scion inlaid in bark and nailed to wood.

Usually the buds on scions of a bridge will start into growth. These growths should be removed early in the season, since it is desirable to establish the scion only as the bridge between root and top. Having growth on the scion itself is counter-productive.

Thousands of trees in commercial orchards have been saved by timely bridge grafting. The procedure is not difficult and can be used to advantage by home gardeners. Obviously, these grafts should be protected from future damage by mice and rabbits. Since the tissues on grafts are more tender than those of the older tree, these animals are especially attracted to them. Keep grass and weeds away from the bases of trees by hoeing, especially into the fall. Wire guards around the tree trunks and pushed into the soil will normally prevent mouse injury.

The original injured stem or tree trunk has one last function to perform — to physically support the tree. It need not be treated in any way to protect it from rotting. Its function is only temporary. The bridges will take over not only the life function of transport of water and nutrients from root to top and the downward movement of leaf-manufactured carbohydrates from top to root but also the physical support function. Often bridges will "grow over" the dead center trunk so that the latter becomes barely visible or is completely masked.

Most failures in bridge-grafting are due to the following reasons: the operation was done too far ahead of the start of spring growth; the grafts were not placed in good live bark either below or above the girdled area; the scion wood used was not dormant; the scion wood was too small or not vigorous, or was partially dried out; the wounds were not properly waxed; there was subsequent rodent or mechanical damage to the bridges.

Inarch Graft

A tree girdled below ground as well as at the surface (usually by mice) can be saved by inarching.

This is done by planting small trees around the tree base and grafting their tops to the trunk of the injured tree. In this method, a piece of bark is removed from the tree trunk above the injured area just wide enough to contain the small tree stem. A slice is cut from one side of the top of the seedling tree and this is placed against the area of the injured tree where the bark was removed and fastened securely with brads. The cambium layers are thus joined.

The tops of the seedlings above the grafts can be left until the grafts have "taken" but then are removed flush with the top of the grafted spot.

All growth developing along the scion tree stems should be

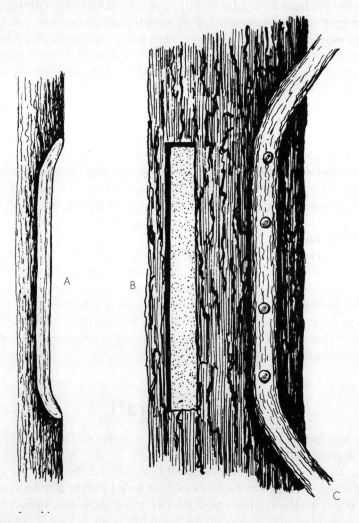

Inarching:
A-seedling with slice cut out, B-channel cut in bark of tree, C-seedling in-arched in the channel and fastened with brads.

removed. Grafts should be made about every four inches around the tree trunk, thus requiring the planting of several seedling trees. All exposed cuts are covered with protective coating as already described.

Whip or Tongue Graft

This graft is suited to cases where the scion and the stock are approximately equal in size and particularly for top-working young apple and pear trees to different varieties of apple or pear.

Uniform sloping cuts are made "to match" on both scion and stock. Also on both, slits are cut beginning at a point one-third the distance from the "toe" (sharp end) to the "heel." The two are then pushed together. If the scion is smaller than the stock, it must be set

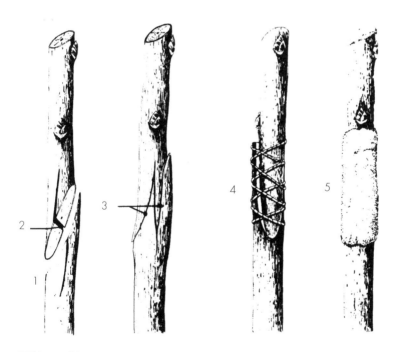

Whip grafting:
1-scion and stock with diagonal cuts, 2-a tongue is cut, 3-cambium layers of stock and scion must come in contact at least on one side, 4-tied with string, 5-cut surfaces waxed

on one side to secure adequate cambial contact at the tongues. This graft is best tied and of course waxed.

Failures with this graft are often due to making the sloping cuts too short, improper placing of the slits, and failure to press the tongues in deeply enough.

Stub Graft

This graft is useful in making over a tree top by grafting many small branches and leaving the main tree branches intact. Fruiting is less interfered with than in using cleft grafts. It is used on the smaller branches less than ¾-inch in diameter. A scion with five to seven buds is cut with a short wedge at the lower end. A diagonal cut is made near the base of the branch to be replaced but not more than half way through a small branch. Pulling the branch down carefully will open the cut. The lower scion end is inserted into this cut. The

Stug grafting:
A-scion, B-scion placed in diagonal cut on top of limb near its base, C-limb cut close to scion, D-wound waxed

branch or lateral is then cut off as close as possible to the scion and all cut surfaces waxed.

No nailing or tying is needed. If dormant scions are available, grafting can be done over a period of six weeks in early spring.

Oblique Side Graft

This is a variation of the stub graft and can be used for about the same purposes, especially for small branches not over ¾-inch in diameter. It can be done quite rapidly. Scions are cut to a one-inch

Oblique side grafting:
A and B-scion, C-making cut in bark of stock, D-scion in place, E-wound covered

sharp wedge. An oblique cut is made in the tree limb and not more than a quarter of the way through it. The scion is inserted by pushing into proper position for cambial contact. No nailing or tying is needed. The original limb is then removed just above the insertion and the cut surface and union area are waxed.

Budding

Budding is a form of grafting in which a single bud rather than a piece of shoot or stem (scion) is inserted into the stock. It is used extensively by nurserymen in the propagation of new fruit trees and many other plants.

Most fruit trees are started as single buds, budded on lined out (closely planted in rows) nursery stock seedlings or vegetatively propagated clones in large commercial nurseries. This allows

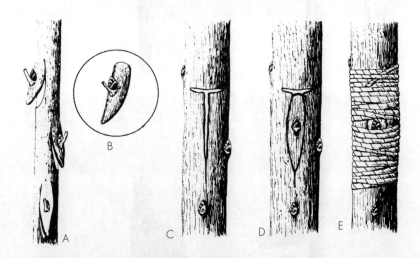

Budding (bud-grafting):
A-budstick, a shoot with leaves cut off and the shield buds made ready;
B-single bud; C-stock with T-cut; D-bud pushed into bark incision;
E-bud tied in with rubber band or string.

chosen varieties to be propagated on specific rootstocks. This is especially important in producing dwarf and semi-dwarf trees which require specialized dwarfing rootstocks.

Budding also is useful in topworking fruit trees, including peaches and other stone fruits (also see Whip Graft and Stub Graft sections). Unlike apples and pears, the wood of peach, plum, and cherry does not split nicely for cleft grafting where as budding is more readily done, especially when the bark "slips" well.

The time for budding is not in early spring, as with most grafting, but in summer, usually in August and September, when the bark of the stock lifts readily.

In the latitude of the northwest, Wisconsin, Michigan, New York, and New England, the suitable dates are generally July 10 to August 10 for apple and pear, August 1 to September 1 for cherry and plum, and August 15 to September 10 for peach. The dates are

Budding:
1-bud tied with raffia, 2-after removal of ties, 3-bud growth (shoot) tied to stock for stability (usually not necessary), 4-stub cut back to point of budding.

somewhat earlier in more southern areas and may vary considerably in particular seasons.

The important consideration here is that the bark on the stock to be budded "slips" easily, indicating cambial cellular activity. If the bark does not lift freely and cleanly from the wood, budding will be largely unsuccessful. Proper timing also is dependent on full maturation of buds on *current* season's shoots. These are the buds used in budding. They will form a union with the stock but will not normally grow out until the next spring.

Vigorous terminal shoots are cut for budsticks (bud source) and the leaves are cut off before any wilting occurs, leaving a quarter-inch or so of petiole (leaf stem) for easy handling of each bud. The hard, plump buds in the middles of the shoots are usually chosen. Those from the upper and lower portions are not used, the former begin too immature and the latter small and weak.

With a sharp budding or pocket knife with rounded blade, a T-shaped cut is made in the bark on the upper side of the stock or limb. The top of the T often is made first. Then the vertical cut is made by drawing the knife upward lightly from a point about an inch below. The bark flaps are opened slightly, by a twisting motion with the knife, to receive the bud.

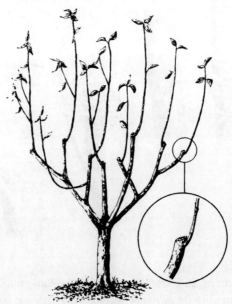

Young apple tree which had been budded in the main branches shows one year's shoot growth from the buds. Top working is thus accomplished.

The bud is cut from the budstick by a shallow slicing cut from ¼-inch below to ¼-above the bud. This "shield" (bud with attached bark below and above it) is then inserted upright into the bark opening by holding the cut leaf stem and pushing down so that it fits snugly against the cambium of the stock. The inserted bud is tied in place by wrapping with rubber strips, string or raffia. No waxing is needed.

Normally the union is achieved and the bud remains dormant until the following spring. Then the limb or stock is cut off close above it without disturbing the union. If raffia or string was used to tie the bud, this must be cut before this time, (usually about three weeks after budding) to avoid tissue injury and actual girdling. Usually, ties are cut two or four weeks after budding since they are unnecessary and serve no further purpose after the bud has united with the stock. Special rubber strips are easy to use and rarely cause injurious constriction even if left on, due to their elastic nature.

Ten Essentials of
Successful Grafting and Budding

1. Have a reason for grafting or budding and a sincere desire to succeed. This means planning ahead regarding scions and buds, tools and supplies since proper timing is essential for satisfactory results.

2. Use only sharp and clean tools, especially the knife, saw, and shears.

3. The scion (or bud) and the stock must be compatible, that is, capable of forming a successful union when joined together under suitable conditions. Grafting and budding are usually confined to closely related plants, for example, one variety of apple on another, but not apple on peach; pear on pear but not on peach; cherry on cherry but not on apple, etc. Grafting is most successful with pome fruits — apple, pear, quince. Budding is successful with all fruits and is the principal method of grafting for stone fruits — peach, cherry, plum, apricot.

4. Grafting should be done at the proper season, usually in early spring. Often, failures have been found to be due to late season grafting attempts, even after trees have leafed out, and using scions not completely dormant. The answer is simply "don't do it," unless you just want to experiment which, if course, can be fun in itself.

   Budding is done in mid or late summer using mature buds found on current season shoots.

5. Don't let scions and buds dry out prior to use. Keep scion and scion bud wood moist and cool. Moist is the real key. Keep out of direct sunlight as much as possible. Do not use scions that have been exposed to drying conditions to any appreciable extent.

6. Scions from the previous season's shoot growth must be dormant when used in grafting. This usually means collection and storing of scion wood prior to spring growth of threes and prior to the actual grafting, although scions can be cut and used for grafting the same day during a short period in early spring. In budding, dormant buds are taken from current season's shoots, which dictates summer timing of this operation. Usually, buds are obtained and used for budding within a short time, often the same day.

7. The cambiums of the scion (or the bud) and the stock must be in intimate contact for union to proceed, with the cells of each dividing and redividing in normal growth processes. The two parts thus become as one.

8. Grafting wounds must be protected from drying out by the use of a proper dressing compound, usually a hand wax or an asphalt-water emulsion preparation. In budding, immediate and proper tying of the buds prevents drying out and waxing is not needed.

9. Nails or brads used in bridge grafting should be very small in diameter to avoid splitting the scions.

10. All grafting and budding should be followed up by inspection and attention to details such as timely pruning of unwanted growths, protection from rodent or other damage, and removal of ties (in budding). Scions should proceed to grow as soon as weather conditions are suitable and the

buds will develop into shoots. Be sure the wax dressing continues to give needed protection from drying out of tissues. Rewaxing sometimes is needed. In summer budding, successful buds will grow out the following season. Competing buds growing from the stock should be kept rubbed or pruned off since they would provide competition and often excessive shading.

Ten Most-Asked Questions About Grafting

Question: What is the difference between grafting and budding?

Answer: In grafting, a scion or piece of wood with several buds is used. In budding a single bud is used.

Question: Is grafting so difficult that only experts can do it?

Answer: No. Anyone with a green thumb can do it. The same statement goes for budding.

Question: Can I graft any time of the year?

Answer: No. Most grafting is done in the spring, just before trees begin to leaf out. Budding is done in mid to late summer.

Question: Can I graft or bud apples on my pear tree?

Answer: Not common, please refer to page 5, 1st paragraph.

Question: Will a graft of McIntosh on a Delicious tree bear apples that have some resemblance to Delicious?

Answer: No. No matter what variety the stock is, the grafted scion or budded bud of McIntosh will produce typical McIntosh apples.

Question: Can a large apple tree be topworked or changed over to another variety by grafting?

Answer: Yes, but the tree should be in good vigor and health and not too old. Topworking a large tree is a big job and often is done progressively over a period of two to three years.

Question: What is the most important cause of failure of grafting or budding?

Answer: Probably letting the scion or bud dry out too much before the operation, or afterwards with inadequate waxing. Another important reason is improper timing.

Question: Is waxing really important in grafting?

Answer: Yes. The reason is that the tissues of both stock and scion must be protected from drying out so that cells will continue to grow and divide. This protection must last until union is achieved.

Question: Why is the cambium important?

Answer: The cambium is the living tissue between the inner bark and the wood that produces the growth that increases the thickness of a woody stem (annual rings). The active cambium cells of stock and scion must be in contact if union is to take place in a graft or bud.

Question: Is grafting important in commercial fruit tree nurseries?

Answer: Yes, and budding (a form of grafting) is the principal method of growing trees for planting by both large fruit growers and backyard orchardists. Grafting is basic to nursery culture.